Exoplanets

SEYMOUR SIMON

HARPER

An Imprint of HarperCollins*Publishers*

To Caroline Herschel, who worked alongside her brother William to discover the planet Uranus . . . and to all the anonymous women scientists of the past who searched the stars for new planets

Special thanks to Mark Miesch

PHOTO AND ART CREDITS: page 2: © ESO/L. Calçada; page 4: © NASA, ESA, and M. Kornmesser (ESO); page 7: © NASA, ESA, and Hubble Heritage Team (STScI/ AURA, Acknowledgment: T. Do, A.Ghez (UCLA), V. Bajaj (STScI); page 8: © NASA/ JPL-Caltech; page 11: © ESO; pages 12-13: © NASA/Kepler Mission/Wendy Stenzel; pages 14-15: © ESA, NASA, and L. Calçada (ESO for STScI); pages 16-17: © Robin Dienel, Carnegie Institution for Science; page 18: © ESO; page 21: © NASA Ames/JPL-Caltech; pages 22-23: © NASA Goddard/Chris Gunn; pages 24-25: © ESO/M. Kornmesser; pages 26-27: © ESO/B. Tafreshi; pages 28-29: Walk-through nebula concept model for the SETI Institute, 2011. Design and photograph by Geoff Puckett; pages 30-31: © Dr. Seth Shostak/Science Source; page 31 top: © SPL/ Science Source; page 33: © Tatiana Plakhova; page 34: © mscomelius/Thinkstock; page 37: © Ralwel/Thinkstock; pages 38-39: © AstroStar/Shutterstock

Library of Congress Control Number: 2016963709
ISBN 978-0-06-247058-4 (trade bdg.) — ISBN 978-0-06-247057-7 (pbk.)

17 18 19 20 21 SCP 10 9 8 7 6 5 4 3 2 1
First Edition
❖

Author's Note

From a young age, I was interested in animals, space, my surroundings—all the natural sciences. When I was a teenager, I became the president of a nationwide junior astronomy club with a thousand members. After college, I became a classroom teacher for nearly twenty-five years while also writing articles and books for children on science and nature even before I became a full-time writer. My experience as a teacher gives me the ability to understand how to reach my young readers and get them interested in the world around us.

I've written more than 300 books, and I've thought a lot about different ways to encourage interest in the natural world, as well as how to show the joys of nonfiction. When I write, I use comparisons to help explain unfamiliar ideas, complex concepts, and impossibly large numbers. I try to engage your senses and imagination to set the scene and to make science fun. For example, in *Penguins*, I emphasize the playful nature of these creatures on the very first page by mentioning how penguins excel at swimming and diving. I use strong verbs to enhance understanding. I make use of descriptive detail and ask questions that anticipate what you may be thinking (sometimes right at the start of the book).

Many of my books are photo-essays, which use extraordinary photographs to amplify and expand the text, creating different and engaging ways of exploring nonfiction. You'll also find a glossary, an index, and website and research recommendations in most of my books, which make them ideal for enhancing your reading and learning experience. As William Blake wrote in his poem, I want my readers "to see a world in a grain of sand, / And a heaven in a wild flower, / Hold infinity in the palm of your hand, / And eternity in an hour."

Seymour Simon

Illustration of planetary systems, like our solar system, in the Milky Way

Most of you remember the story of Goldilocks. She went for a walk and came upon a house in the woods. She knocked, and when no one answered she went inside. In the kitchen, there were three bowls of porridge. The first was too hot, the second was too cold, but the last bowl was just right, and she ate it all up. The same thing happened with three chairs and three beds. One chair was too large and the other too small; one bed was too hard and the other too soft. But the third chair and the third bed were just right for Goldilocks.

Scientists are looking for "Goldilocks" planets in their search for distant Earths in the Milky Way galaxy. The distant planets have to be just right—not too hot nor too cold, not too large nor too small. They have to be like our planet Earth, about the right temperature and the right size to possibly support life as we know it.

Planets found circling stars other than our own star, the sun, are called exoplanets. In the last twenty years, scientists have found more than 3,000 exoplanets circling over 2,000 distant stars. Many are very unlike any planets in our **solar system**, but some are Goldilocks, or **habitable**, exoplanets similar to Earth where we might find alien life. Our sun is one of at least 100 billion stars in the Milky Way, a barred spiral **galaxy** about 100,000 **light-years** across. One light-year is the distance that light travels in one year. Light moves at 186,000 miles every second (300,000 kilometers a second). One light-year is 5.88 trillion miles (9.5 trillion km). That's more than 63,000 times the distance of Earth to the sun, so 100,000 light-years is a huge number in miles or kilometers.

Here's another way to think about it—imagine the Milky Way galaxy is the whole United States of America. Our whole solar system then would be the size of a quarter coin placed on the United States. Meanwhile, the sun would be only a microscopic speck of dust on that scale. The stars in the Milky Way galaxy are located in a pinwheel pattern with four major arms, and we live about two-thirds of the way up one of them.

Hubble Space Telescope photograph of the heart of the Milky Way galaxy

Illustration of a pulsar planet system

Many, if not most, stars host their own families of planets. Based on observations, scientists predict that there should be about one Goldilocks, Earth-size planet in the habitable zone of each red dwarf star. Red dwarf stars are by far the most common type of star in the galaxy. Other stars that are more similar to our own sun might have even more habitable planets **orbiting** them. That means the Milky Way galaxy might contain billions of alien planets, and a good number of these might support life. There are about 7 billion people in the world. There might be eight or nine alien planets per person for the entire human population on Earth!

Even before the first exoplanets were confirmed in the 1990s, many **astronomers** predicted their existence. That's because scientists think that our solar system began as a spinning cloud of gas and dust. The cloud slowly collapsed under its own **gravity** and formed the sun and the planets. Astronomers reasoned that planets must be common around sunlike stars.

At first, astronomers searched for exoplanets around stars like our sun. But the first confirmed discovery of an exoplanet was around a pulsar (a rapidly spinning dead supernova, a star that once exploded) called PSR B1257+12. The next discovery of a planet orbiting a sunlike star was 51 Pegasi b, a Jupiter-size world twenty times closer to its sun than Earth is to our own sun.

There are eight planets in our solar system. The first four planets closest to the sun are small and rocky (Mercury, Venus, Earth, and Mars). The next four planets are big and gassy (Jupiter, Saturn, Uranus, and Neptune). But some of the exoplanets in solar systems that have been discovered so far are not at all like the familiar planets in our solar system. There is a giant exoplanet, much bigger than Jupiter, orbiting a sun so closely that they are practically on top of each other. There is another exoplanet circling two stars in a solar system far away.

In the mid–1990s, the only exoplanets that could be detected were very big, much bigger than Jupiter, the largest planet in our solar system. One of the early ways astronomers looked for exoplanets is called the radial velocity method. They looked for a small wobble in a star that might be caused by the gravitational pull of a planet orbiting that star. Then, as computers and **telescopes** got more advanced, astronomers began finding smaller planets. Many exoplanets have been discovered in this way. However, this method only works well for Jupiter-size gassy planets and larger, and these are unlikely to have life, unless they have a habitable moon.

Illustration of a Jupiter-size exoplanet and its sun

Illustration of the Kepler space telescope searching for
different types of exoplanets

In recent years, scientists began using the transit method, which looks for the slight dimming of a star that would be caused by a planet passing in front of the star. Using this method, scientists look for Earth-size planets and also for gases such as water vapor, which might show the possibility of life.

Nowadays, there are more than several thousand exoplanets that have been discovered by a single telescope using the transit method. The Kepler space telescope, which went into orbit around the sun in 2009, has confirmed more than half of the known exoplanets to date and spotted over 4,000 more waiting to be confirmed.

Kepler was named after a famous astronomer, Johannes Kepler. The space telescope was designed to look for possible habitable planets, and it has discovered a treasury of different types of exoplanets. Besides gas giants and Earth-like planets, Kepler found a new category known as **super-Earths**, planets between the size of Earth and Neptune. Some of these are in the Goldilocks zone in their solar systems, and scientists are studying how life might develop on these giant planets.

After a few years Kepler stopped working because of a malfunction that prevented it from pointing at a star without drifting off course. But scientists devised a remarkable solution. They used the pressure of sunlight to steer the spaceship so that it could continue to explore. A new mission, called K2, is providing even more results. In May 2016, the scientists of Kepler announced 1,284 verified new planets, many more planets than had been verified before. Thanks to Kepler and K2, scientists now know that there are probably more planets than stars in the galaxy.

The hunt for new exoplanets is gaining speed. A new way of finding an exoplanet is called direct imaging, photographing a planet directly. Scientists must first use an instrument to block the light from the star, revealing the dimmer light reflected by the exoplanet. In 2008, scientists announced the discovery of Fomalhaut b, an exoplanet imaged in visible light. On the same day, another team of scientists, using infrared light, announced the discovery of a solar system of four planets circling a star. Since then, direct imaging has been used with other earlier methods to explore for new exoplanets.

Illustration of a Jupiter-size planet circling the star Fomalhaut

Exoplanets come in a huge variety of sizes and distances from the stars they orbit. Many are gigantic planets traveling close to their parent suns. Some are icy, circling far from the suns at the center of their solar systems. Some are gassy, much like the outer giant planets in our own solar system. Others are rocky, like Earth and the inner planets in our solar system.

Here are just a few of the amazing exoplanets we have discovered:

• **Proxima b:** A rocky planet in the Goldilocks zone, orbiting Proxima Centauri, the closest star to our sun. Although it is the closest exoplanet to Earth in the entire **universe**, it doesn't mean that it's *that* close. It's 4.2 light-years away; that's 266,000 times the distance from

Earth to the sun. Still, scientists are working to create ultrafast small spacecraft that would reach the planet twenty years after launch and beam home images.

- **91 Aquarii b:** In our solar system, the planets circle one star, the sun. But there are many solar systems that have two or more stars at the center. Think of it as Star Wars' Tatooine, the home planet of Luke Skywalker, which had two suns. 91 Aquarii b is an exoplanet part of a triple star system, so it has three stars.

- **Trappist-1:** About 40 light-years away, seven Earth-size planets orbit a dwarf star, with three in the Goldilocks zone. Most of the Trappist-1 planets are also rocky like Earth. The planets are close enough for scientists to begin to find out if the planets have atmospheres and water on them.

Illustration of three giant worlds orbiting twin suns

Earth lies in the Goldilocks habitable zone of our star, the sun. Beyond this zone, our planet would probably be too frozen for life. Closer to the sun, the planet would probably be too hot. The perfect Goldilocks planet wouldn't necessarily be home to intelligent creatures. But it would have the potential for some kind of life to exist, if even **microbes**.

The earliest thinking was that in order for a planet to have the possibility of life it had to be at a certain distance from a star that would allow for ocean water, critical for life on Earth. That meant that a planet had to be at just the right distance from its sun to have temperatures between the freezing and boiling points of water. But new calculations include many other factors, including the "greenhouse effect" of a planet's atmosphere. That makes the boundaries of the habitable zone much fuzzier, giving many more exoplanets the chance to potentially contain living things.

We now know that the galaxy is teeming with exoplanets, many of which are Earth-size or super-Earths and appear to be orbiting their parent star in the habitable zone. Each star has a different habitable zone. More massive stars than our sun are hotter and blaze with **radiation**, so the habitable zone is farther out. Stars that are smaller and cooler have habitable zones closer and tighter.

One study by the NASA Exoplanet Science Institute analyzed the location of a planet called Kepler-69c and the habitable zone of its sun. The planet is a bit less than two times the size of Earth and lies just inside the inner edge of the zone. That makes it too hot, more of a super-Venus than a super-Earth. It turns out that many exoplanets are super-Venus–like planets rather than super-Earth–like planets.

Kepler-69 System

Habitable zone

69c   69b

Mercury   Venus   Earth   Mars

Our Solar System

Planets and orbits to scale

Illustration of the habitable zones of the Kepler-69 system and our solar system

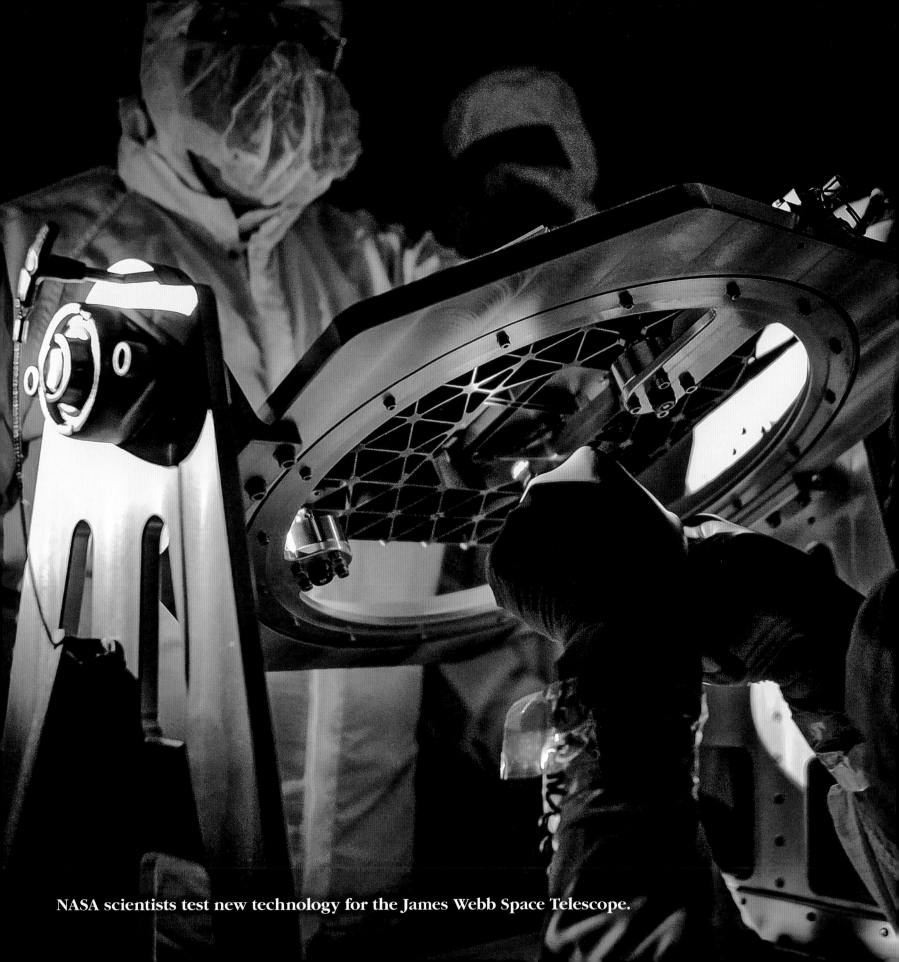

NASA scientists test new technology for the James Webb Space Telescope.

The habitable zone of a star also depends upon the chemistry of a planet. For example, some kinds of gas **molecules** in a planet's atmosphere will absorb a certain amount of sunlight and radiate the rest back out into space. How much of the energy is absorbed could mean the difference between an ocean of water and a sea of boiling lava. Astronomers would like to learn much more about the atmosphere of Goldilocks planets. NASA's 2018 James Webb Space Telescope will bring them closer to this goal.

But before you sign up for a vacation on an exoplanet, keep in mind that there are many other factors that make for pleasant ocean beaches or burning hot deserts. Eruptions from stars, called flares, can destroy the atmosphere of a planet. On the other hand, water is a pretty good shield for radiation, so maybe life could thrive in alien oceans. We still have a lot to learn about the possibilities of life on distant worlds.

Illustration of the Gliese 667 system from one of its exoplanets

epler and other observatories have found many exoplanets that may be capable of supporting some kind of alien life. Here are some that have been discovered:

• **Gliese 667Cc:** This is a super-Earth, at least 4.5 times the mass of Earth, orbiting a red dwarf star, Gliese 667C. The planet orbits its sun in only twenty-eight days, but the star is much cooler than the sun. If the planet had liquid water on the surface, the temperature would be about 90°F (30°C). That might allow for life but there are many complications, so no one knows for sure.

• **Kepler-442b, Kepler-438b, Kepler-62f:** These three exoplanets orbit red dwarf stars that are smaller and cooler than our sun.

Swirling stars in a time-lapse photograph over the Atacama Large Millimeter Array telescope (ALMA) in the Southern Hemisphere

Are we alone in the universe? Are there exoplanets with intelligent alien life? Are there aliens trying to talk to people on Earth? Would we even understand what they have to say? Is anyone here listening? If we are alone in the universe, then we would be the only intelligence that is able to explore these questions.

But what if the answer is no, we are not alone? Then what? Who else is out there? What are they like? What kind of knowledge do they have? How would they act toward us if they found out we exist? What questions would we ask and what would we tell them?

We have the knowledge and the technology to both send and receive radio signals over vast distances in space. Actually we have been sending out signals for nearly a century, since the early days of radio and television broadcasting. All our programs leak out into space and spread across the galaxy. Perhaps some advanced aliens have listened and are now sending messages to us. The only way to know is to listen. For over fifty years, we have been listening for signals from space.

In 1960, a young radio astronomer named Frank Drake started to conduct the first detailed search for aliens in deep space. He aimed the 85-foot dish of a radio telescope at two nearby sunlike stars. He tuned the radio telescope to listen to signals at a frequency (like a station) that he thought the aliens might use to broadcast.

And so began the Search for Intelligent Life (SETI), an organization dedicated to the search for **extraterrestrial intelligence**. But so far the search has failed to detect a single "hello" from an alien. Why haven't we heard? Pick your own answer: We have looked at only a tiny fraction of the stars in our own galaxy. Would we even know a signal if we saw it? Aliens are not there. They are too far away. They are zoned out watching TV and playing video games and not listening to us. Or they are watching us, laughing at how silly we are and not interested in talking to us. Anything might be possible. We just don't know . . . yet.

Proposed SETI exhibit of what humans would see if they could walk through a nebula

In 1974, Frank Drake created the Arecibo Message (shown above), a simple broadcast sent into space by the Arecibo radio telescope in Puerto Rico. The message encoded several things in binary form (a computer way of speaking): the numbers 1 to 10, the basic chemistry of life on Earth, the double helix structure of the DNA molecule (in all life on Earth), Earth's human population at that time, a graphic of the solar system, a human figure, and a graphic of the Arecibo radio telescope. We don't know if any aliens have received the message. So far no one has replied to Drake's Arecibo Message.

In recent years, a new and expanded search called Breakthrough Listen was begun by a famous physicist, Stephen Hawking. The Breakthrough search seeks to answer questions such as: Are we alone in the universe? Are there other Goldilocks planets in the Milky Way galaxy? Can we make the giant leap to go to the stars? And, most importantly, can humankind think and work together as a whole and act as one world in the endless realm of outer space?

Perhaps life is possible all over the Milky Way galaxy and the hundred billion more galaxies in the universe. Breakthrough Listen will allow scientists to collect as much information in one day as we did in one year before. So we're still listening, but now we're doing more than listening—we're talking too.

Listening to space

Illustration of an imaginary alien spaceship

Some SETI researchers have decided to send out messages to newly discovered exoplanets. They are targeting Earth-size planets in the Goldilocks zone and through "active SETI," which talks as well as listens. We're announcing that we are here and trying to get a conversation started. We have not heard anything yet. Sometimes, we thought we found an interesting signal, but nothing has been verified . . . yet. There may be a bigger problem, though. Some scientists think it's a very bad idea to announce that Earth is listening and wants to talk. Why? Well, there might be bad aliens.

In a petition to stop sending a "hello" message into outer space, twenty-eight scientists and researchers came together to say it was a bad idea. They wrote, "ETI's [Extra Terrestrial Intelligent being] reaction to a message from Earth cannot presently be known . . . it is impossible to predict whether ETI will be benign [friendly] or hostile [unfriendly]."

SETI scientists responded by pointing out that even if there are unfriendly aliens out there, they already know all about us. That's because news programs and other TV and radio broadcasts have been radiating out from Earth for a long time. Advanced alien civilizations might also detect our radar signals and even the lights of large cities on Earth. And these signals can't be recalled. Once sent, they will continue going out in space. But there is another problem. What should we say? And who speaks for Earth? So what do you think? Should we send out messages to space? And what should we say?

So, what are the chances of life on alien worlds? Many astronomers believe that there is probably some form of life on other worlds. Frank Drake thinks there may be at least 10,000 alien civilizations that we could detect if we looked in the right places with the right instruments and right methods. There may be even more than 10,000. Drake goes on to say, "A lot more young ones that don't have the technology and there are older ones that have technology that is so good that they don't waste any energy."

There are so many unknowns about alien planets at this time that we can't even begin to answer many questions. One reason is that even the closest stars are so far away from Earth. For example, going at the speed of today's spaceships that travel to the moon and nearby planets, it would take tens of thousands or hundreds of thousands of years to get to even the closest alien planets.

Artist's image of other planets as seen from an alien world

No one knows for sure how many of these Goldilocks planets actually have life. The reason is we don't know exactly how life began on Earth. Also, how likely is it that simple microbes will eventually become complex life and intelligent aliens? Again, we have no idea.

So why are we even looking? We're looking for answers because that's what humans do. We are curious about our world and our surroundings. We are curious about space and the universe. We have a thirst for knowledge. And unlike ordinary thirst, our curiosity is never satisfied. Each answer brings forth countless new questions. Our quest for knowledge always continues, and you are part of that journey every time you look up at the night sky and wonder.

GLOSSARY

Astronomer—A person skilled in astronomy who scientifically studies the solar system, the stars, and the universe.

Extraterrestrial intelligence (ETI)—Alien life-forms that can communicate across space.

Galaxy—One of millions of star systems, each containing billions of stars and planets and clouds of dust and gas.

Gravity—The force that attracts things to the Earth, the moon, a planet, or a star. Gravity is what causes people and objects to have weight on Earth.

Habitable—Capable of being lived in.

Light-year—A unit of length in astronomy equal to the distance that light travels in one year in a vacuum, or about 5.88 trillion miles.

Microbe—Microorganism, germ.

Molecule—A group of two or more atoms linked together by sharing electrons in a chemical bond.

Nebula—A huge cloud of stars or dust and gases in deep space beyond the solar system.

Orbit—The curved path of a celestial object or spacecraft around a star, planet, or moon.

Radiation—Energy radiated in the form of waves or particles.

Solar system—The sun and other objects that revolve around it, including planets, moons, comets, and asteroids.

Super-Earths—Extrasolar planets with a mass higher than Earth but less than

the mass of an ice giant planet such as Neptune.

Telescope—An instrument in which an arrangement of lenses and/or other devices are designed to make distant objects appear near.

Universe—All the matter and energy in space, now and in the past, including the Milky Way, all the other galaxies, the stars, the planets, and everything else that exists.

INDEX

READ MORE ABOUT IT

Seymour Simon's website
www.seymoursimon.com

NASA
https://exoplanets.nasa.gov
https://exoplanets.nasa.gov
/galleries/exoplanet-travel-bureau/

European Space Agency
www.esa.int/esaKIDSen/
SEM3NFXPXPF_LifeinSpace_0
.html